Haunting Memories

Haunting Memories

Echoes and Images of Tennessee's Past

Hand-Tinted Photographs by
Christine P. Patterson

Text by
Wilma Dykeman

The University of Tennessee Press • Knoxville

RAINBO
IS
Good
BREAD

First Edition.

The paper in this book meets the minimum requirements of the American National Standard for Permanence of Paper for Printed Library Materials. ♾ The binding materials have been chosen for strength and durability.

Library of Congress Cataloging-in-Publication Data

Patterson, Christine P. (Christine Penrose), 1961–
Haunting memories : echoes and images of Tennessee's past: hand-tinted photographs / by Christine P. Patterson; text by Wilma Dykeman. —1st ed.
p. cm.
ISBN 0-87049-930-0 (cloth: alk. paper)
1. Tennessee—Pictorial works. 2. Tennessee—Description and travel. I. Dykeman, Wilma. II. Title.
F437.P38 1996
976.8'0022'2—dc20 95-41759
CIP

Contents

Preface

This enchanting book unites the talents of two Tennessee residents, photographer, Christine Patterson, and poet and historian, Wilma Dykeman. Their collaboration presents an uncommon view of Tennessee's history. We are given not merely historical reference, nor geographic pinpoints on a map. The images captured here, and the words which accompany them, invite us to peer closely and listen intently, with our imaginations poised. These buildings beckon us, as though they seek to unburden themselves of the secrets held within their walls for many years.

Some we may recognize. They are the landmarks we visited as children. Others stand forgotten, visited only by time. Though fortune may conspire to preserve some remnants of our past, many are vanishing. Long abandoned by their caretakers, they disappear into obscurity, irretrievably lost.

It was a desire to conserve these images that speak of our history, and to manifest the spirit of a bygone era, that compelled the photographer to embark on a personal expedition. It began with brief forays down back roads into the small towns and counties that together connect the many diverse regions of Tennessee. By journey's end, she had crisscrossed the entire state, and traveled an astounding twenty thousand miles.

Often surprised by the distance she had traveled, Ms. Patterson stopped frequently to explore empty buildings that stood abandoned near the roadside. Battered by wind, and warped by exposure to the sun, they endured the unending erosion of time. Beneath the vaulted ceiling of the Century Old Baptist Church, the people of a community had prayed. Years ago farmers had gathered at Blowing Cave Mill and traded stories to the sound of the millstone grinding wheat into flour. A child had tarried on the dusty sunlit porch of Sampson's General Store. Ms. Patterson was drawn to these structures by what she has described as a palpable energy that surrounded them. The spirits of their former inhabitants seemed to linger in the shadows, waiting to be recognized.

Her wish to give tangible expression to this aura, led Ms. Patterson to transcend the limits of conventional photography and experiment with unusual film. She chose Kodak black-and-white infrared film for its unique properties. Infrared film is often used in scientific photography for its ability to enhance images that are invisible to the human eye. Sunlit objects or those which absorb heat, and plant material, which contains chlorophyll, appear very bright on infrared film. Objects unseen by the naked eye emerge with startling clarity. More recently, photographers have used infrared film for its artistic characteristics. Though it is difficult to work with (it must be constantly refrigerated and handled in total darkness) the creative freedom it affords the photographer is worth the care required for its preservation. Infrared is capable of producing phantasmal images with eerie and dreamlike qualities.

Because the film is also sensitive to blue, red, and violet light rays, the photographer used a standard medium-red filter to block unwanted light sources that may have competed on the exposure. In some instances, she applied petroleum jelly to the filter to obscure modern-day intrusions such as telephone poles, automobiles, or current architecture. The petroleum jelly also served to spread out light as it was picked up on the film. This uncustomary technique creates a swirling visual effect that makes the photographs move. We see an example in the photograph of the Cowan Railroad. Though this locomotive has been still for many years, in the photograph it appears to have just arrived screeching into the station.

As interesting as the photographer's unusual choice of film, is the artistic process by which she achieved the final images. Ms. Patterson developed each photograph individually in her photography lab. She enlarged the initial prints then reprinted them onto a luminous tapestry-style paper with a fiber base resembling canvas. She then used a bleach and toner combination to produce a sepia tone, a brown-toned print that resembles an old photograph, and enhances the ethereal quality of the image. Once the sepia tones were dry, the assiduous process of hand-tinting began.

Hand-tinting is an artistic process that dates back to the Victorian era. Using watercolors, chalk, and oil mediums, the artist applies color to a black-and-white print. Along with these, Ms. Patterson used the natural elements of cranberries for the vivid red hues contained in their pulp. She produced some of the soft browns by mixing a special paint from ground coffee beans. She painstakingly applied each layer of color over a period of several days.

Though hand-painting to create a dramatic mood, Ms. Patterson always kept a still color photograph at hand to insure that she did not diminish the integrity of her subject. What emerged from the studio were no longer static images, but pictures awash in color. These photographs both delight us in the present and invite us to imagine a scene as it might have been many years ago. They encourage inquisitiveness. And promise a story.

The stories these photographs suggest would not be complete without a voice. When the photographer read Wilma Dykeman's *Tennessee, A History,* she felt an immediate affinity with the writer's keen appreciation of her Tennessee heritage. Ms. Dykeman's prose evoked vivid images in the mind of the photographer, and she believed this gifted writer could bring to her photographs the resonance of poetic interpretation. In October of 1994, she met Ms. Dykeman at the Southern Festival of Books in Nashville, Tennessee, and showed the author samples of her work in progress. Intrigued by the breadth and originality of the collection, Ms. Dykeman agreed to write for the book. Thus the photographer and the writer bound their artistry together to create this beautiful volume.

We are the beneficiaries of their collaboration, for in their vision lies a passageway through which we may journey into the history of Tennessee. These photographs, and the words woven between them, awaken the sleeping traveler within us. We may allow ourselves to be transported into the lives of generations past, through the magic of memory, and the permanence of its echoing voice.

Leigh Hogan Fowkes

Acknowledgments

I would like to thank those that have been supportive and inspirational while I worked on this project:

My husband and best friend, Ed Winter, who gently kept pushing me forward with love and encouragement on those days I wanted to quit.

My family, who cheered me on.

Wilma Dykeman, who was a delight to work with as well as an honor to collaborate with.

Susan Long, who put in countless hours of tedious work in the darkroom and helped me in culling from a hundred images the thirty-six shown in this book.

Cherie Lawson, for all of her boundless energy in typing and filing all of the information accumulated during this project.

Bennett Gallery of Knoxville, for their belief that this project would be a permanent message to Tennesseans and for hosting its initial showing in December of 1993.

Luminos Printmaker's Guild, who have been supporters in this project from the beginning, with their beautiful photographic paper that enhanced each image.

Leigh Hogan Fowkes, my dear childhood friend, who so eloquently put into words in the preface my quest in doing this project.

The University of Tennessee Press, for making this book a reality.

And all my friends and patrons, who have encouraged me and believed in me that this project was something special.

Tennessee, with its magical flavors of culture, music, religion, and geography, would captivate any soul.

Christine P. Patterson

Introduction

"Come," Christine Patterson invites, "and share with me a fresh discovery of the beauty and history that is part of the mountains and meadows, the rivers and villages, the country roads and habitations in hidden corners of Tennessee."

"Look," Christine Patterson says, "and see anew familiar objects that hold meaning beyond their utilitarian purposes."

"Welcome," Christine Patterson says, "to sunlight on still waters, storm clouds gathering above Shiloh, past and prophecy all one in this net of time."

I accepted her invitation, and this book is the result of our collaboration.

It should be understood at once that this choice of subjects was exclusively hers. Most of these pictures were begun, or finished, before we even met. Both the originality and unity of the collection are due to the viewpoint she brought to bear during travels across the state.

Our association had a clumsy beginning.

Early in 1994 friends urged me to attend exhibits of the work of a young Knoxville artist, Christine Patterson, whose photographs were enhanced by a special tinting process she had developed. A heavy schedule of speaking engagements and travel made it impossible for me to visit these exhibits. Then, as winter melted into spring, I happened to be in the vicinity of Bennett Gallery and on impulse I stopped by and asked if any Christine Patterson prints or reproductions were available for viewing. There were four.

Later I saw more of her pictures. They spoke to me. When at last we met it developed that my writing had spoken to her. We agreed to bring her photographs and my words together.

We worked separately, yet with a curious affinity for the mood and meaning implicit in each picture. Christine provided me with a selection of the pictures. One at a time I placed them in my most private room, seeking the mood, the spirit, the story within each subject.

My own acquaintance with the scenes and objects Christine captured with her camera was the result of a half-century spent in quest of both the past and present character of our state. In local, regional, and national archives I had pursued the facts and paradoxes of our history. Explorations across every county in Tennessee by various modes of travel along roads ranging from weed-choked footpaths to spacious interstates had left me acquainted with the antiquities and folklore Christine gathered.

There was another factor, however, beyond my compatibility with the book's subject matter, that influenced my decision to lay aside other work and write accompanying passages for these pictures.

I was intrigued by the eclectic choice of

subjects. Here was surprise and delight. More often than not, *what* the artist saw was less important than *how* she saw it. Her pictures were not only descriptive. They were also powerfully evocative. No concessions to achieving geographic balance or historical comprehensiveness had diverted Christine from her personal vision. A scene was not merely pretty or striking. It was also reminder of the ways of survival in certain times and places, memory of the pleasure and struggle, the dreams or disasters that helped distinguish each specific locale. An object was not simply an interesting artifact preserved from the past. It spoke of lives of the few who were renowned or the many who remain unknown, each filling a role in history's pageant.

As she collected photographs Christine recorded interviews with people who shared their knowledge of a local scene, event, characters in a specific situation. (These interviews are identified or partially incorporated at the end of the book.) But the very nature of her art released my words from becoming perfunctory descriptions of a picture's contents and permitted them voyage into the realm of poetic understanding.

My text, therefore, with only a few exceptions, does not focus on geographic locations or historical explanations of Christine's subjects. It is not intended to help someone pinpoint these places on a map—again, with a few exceptions. The desire is to evoke that sense of past and present, harmony and discord, that can stir memories, arouse pleasure, increase appreciation for the rich variety in the world of nature and human nature not only in Tennessee but elsewhere. Universal revelations are ever in our daily routine and its accepted details.

Perhaps those who enter these pages, wherever they have lived or ventured, will find a kinship in simple things, a shared pleasure in discovering familiar yesterdays afresh, joy in creating the voices of memory.

In these pages a bridge may be more than a means of crossing water or a ravine. It can represent passage from one way of knowing life to another kind of knowing.

A building can become more than its caption as a school, a barber shop, a courthouse, a cabin or mansion.

Each object harbors responses to the demands, the rewards, the small vanities and endless vitality of life in this place. A kitchen stove means more than heat for cooking, a wagon represents more than transportation. Each suggests roots and outreach, staying-put or moving-on, singly or together.

If that togetherness reaches out from Christine's pictures and my words, from past to present to you—welcome!

Wilma Dykeman

Haunting Memories

Where have they gone?
Where are the voices bright as
morning bird-calls
greeting each other?
"Mornin'"
"Evenin'"
"How's your folks?"
Where have they gone,
leaving the hollow room shuttered
and barred
against the light
that blesses leafy trees and worn planks
on the ever-welcoming porch?
Where have they gone (replaced by
slight, unseasoned perches),
those rocking chairs with split-oak seats
polished by seasons of use
shaped to a storyteller's comfort,
and those straight-backed chairs tilted
against the wall,
inviting time to stand still
while history is spun in remembrance of
laughter, terror, death and love
no less here than everywhere,
lost and real.
Where have they gone—the bread
and words
that filled empty spaces
for a waiting child?

Beauty becomes a haunting memory.
Like music of violin and fragrance of
lilacs
it twines its tendrils around mind and
heart
and will not let go,
resurrected daily in fragile stare of china
doll,
stillness of waiting rocking horse,
shoes in which she ran and frolicked and
stubbed a toe,
and the ready spinning wheel, reminder
of matronly duties yet to come.
Serenely she looks down upon
yesterday that was too brief,
tomorrow that never came.
She was sixteen,
sixth child of the family,
beauty become a haunting presence.

Winter wind assaulted the sturdy logs and stone of the
house—
but it stood.
Summer storms slashed at farm buildings nestled
nearby—
but they held.
The government begun here would be buffeted, too—
but it would endure.

They had crossed the mountains to this land of Western
Waters,
cutting the umbilical bonds to Europe as they built
in this bountiful wild country which had already borne
many white man's names:
British Colony
Tributary to the Indians
Watauga Association
Washington District of North Carolina
Washington County
the State of Franklin
Washington County again

And now, in 1790, ceded by North Carolina to the United
States, it would be
the Territory of the United States South of the River Ohio.
Capital of raw frontier found temporary home on the farm
called Rocky Mount.
Among pastures and cornfields, gardens and forests, animals
wild and tame,
the business of government unfolded:
organizing counties and courts to set boundaries of land and
behavior,
following messages of appointments from distant President
Washington,
answering inquiries from land speculators in the East,
keeping peace with tribes who still looked upon this land as
their Hunting Ground;
daily more to decide, to do.
The government moved on to other capitals.
Those who built here served briefly as host of the state-to-be.
But the weathered logs and well-placed stones they laid remain,
harboring the secret web of wisdom and folly,
selflessness and self-interest, hope and failure
that forever weaves past to present
in the name of history.

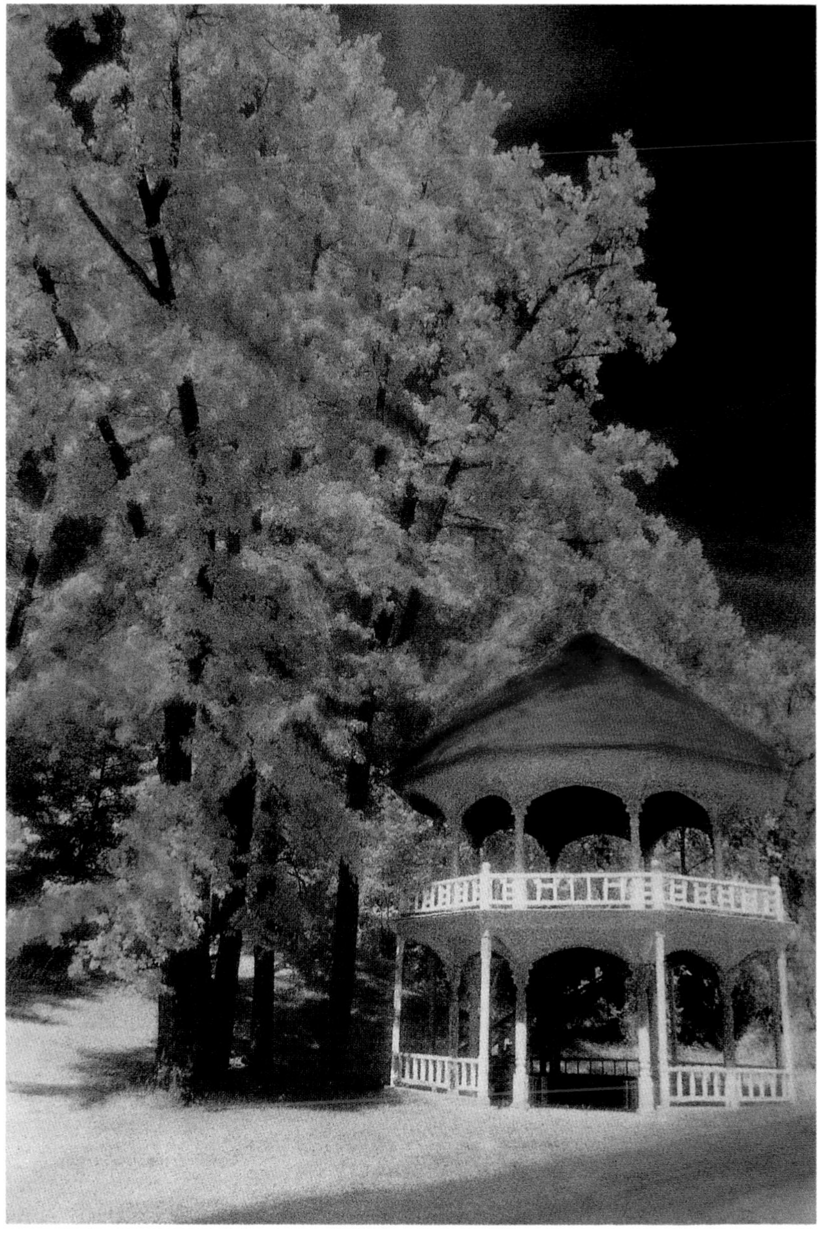

It was always summer there.
  The Springs brought sparkle to the
    eyes,
bounce to every step.
Mornings were for taking the waters
served from silver trays and then in long,
    relaxing baths.
Afternoons were carriage rides through
    the rustic country
and dramatic recitations by a lady
    wearing lavender
who had studied elocution.
Evenings, when moonlight bathed lawn
    and verandahs in magic
or rain curtained the corners in secrecy,
there was dancing, flirting, dreams and
    disappointments,
while patriarchs enjoyed cigars and
    chuckled
at their remembrances of earlier times at
    The Springs
when girls were prettier, days were
    longer, the waters more beneficial.
Summers here for languid ladies and
    attentive gentlemen
were the good life.
For those who served them here
summer at The Springs was a good living.

Sometimes in the soft light of early
evening
she sat down at the keyboard.
Music filled the lonely spaces: marching
songs and waltzes
returned happy moments of her
years
as Sarah Childress Polk,
First Lady of her country.
Laughter followed her ban on alcohol
at the White House social functions,
but her attention was trained on him,
her husband, the President,
whom she often served as secretary
and privy adviser on important issues.
He pushed the boundaries of the nation
until it stretched from Atlantic to
Pacific.
Their companionship stretched
boundaries, too, all unknown,
and when he died three months after
leaving Washington
she survived during forty-two more years,
respected.
Memory, not nostalgia, strengthened
the evenings of her days.

She came early and kindled a fire
in the pot-bellied stove that
sometimes smoked
and brought tears to her eyes.
When the children came she asked a
boy, maybe two,
to carry water from the spring and rinse
the dipper.
Then she looked out at their faces—
scrubbed or dirty,
their feet—well-shod or bare (even in
winter),
looked at the worn, nicked, name-carved
desks,
books unhinged by years of near-death
battering.
But she taught them,
youngest scholars aloud while the older
read silently;
after awhile the smallest ones looked at
pictures of distant lands
and the oldest wrestled with words and
sums
and history in stern facts and dates.
She yearned to kindle respect for
knowledge and sometimes the effort
brought tears to her eyes.

Some people built castles in the air.
He'd build one in Tennessee.
He'd learned about castles and barricades
in books he read.
He'd mapped the world
in his imagination:
Castles of Sir Walter Scott's romances,
Arthur's ramparts on the Cornish coast,
The Moors' Alhambra in Granada,
Teutonic castles strung along the Rhine,
Norman turrets, Inca strongholds,
Crusaders' fortresses on Rhodes.
All bastions against assault
by every invader
save one.
His castle, like all the ones he dreamed of,
empty now.
Only winds and clouds and hovering trees
live on.

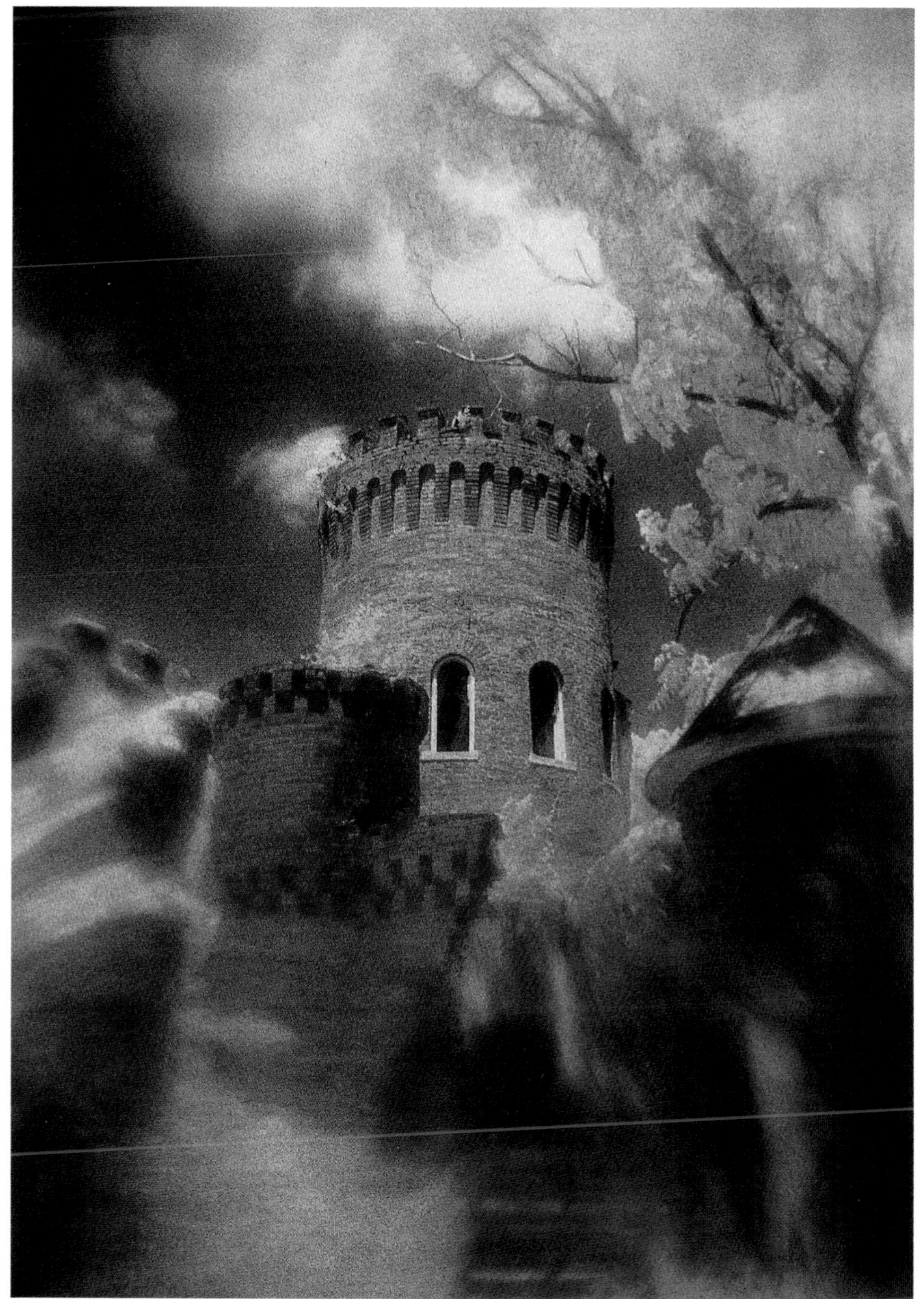

"Mornin' fellers."
"Y'all right today?"
"Reckon I can't complain."
"Last night, yesterday,
you hear what happened?"

First it was a bank,
became a newspaper office,
then found its proper purpose:
a barber shop in fine headquarters
where a fellowship of news opened the
day,
news anchored in neighbors' long
memories.

The scissors click, razors smooth
rough beards, their voices mingle.
"Miss Maudella died four-ten this
mornin'."
Respectfully they listen.
"Nice lady. Pity she never married."
Regretfully they nod.
"Remember the time Jim's balky mule,
old Frank,
passing her farm come upon that
hornet's nest?"
Softly they chuckle.
"Wasn't it her great-grandpa went
west after The War?"

Foreheads wrinkle in disapproval.
"Then her pa and brother died in
that flu epidemic
and her mama took to her bed, plumb
deranged."
Silence bestows compassionate
approval on Miss Maudella.
Facts and figures lie catalogued in the
courthouses.
But here, in daily gathering places,
beyond the ledgers,
hear the ready archives of our daily lives.

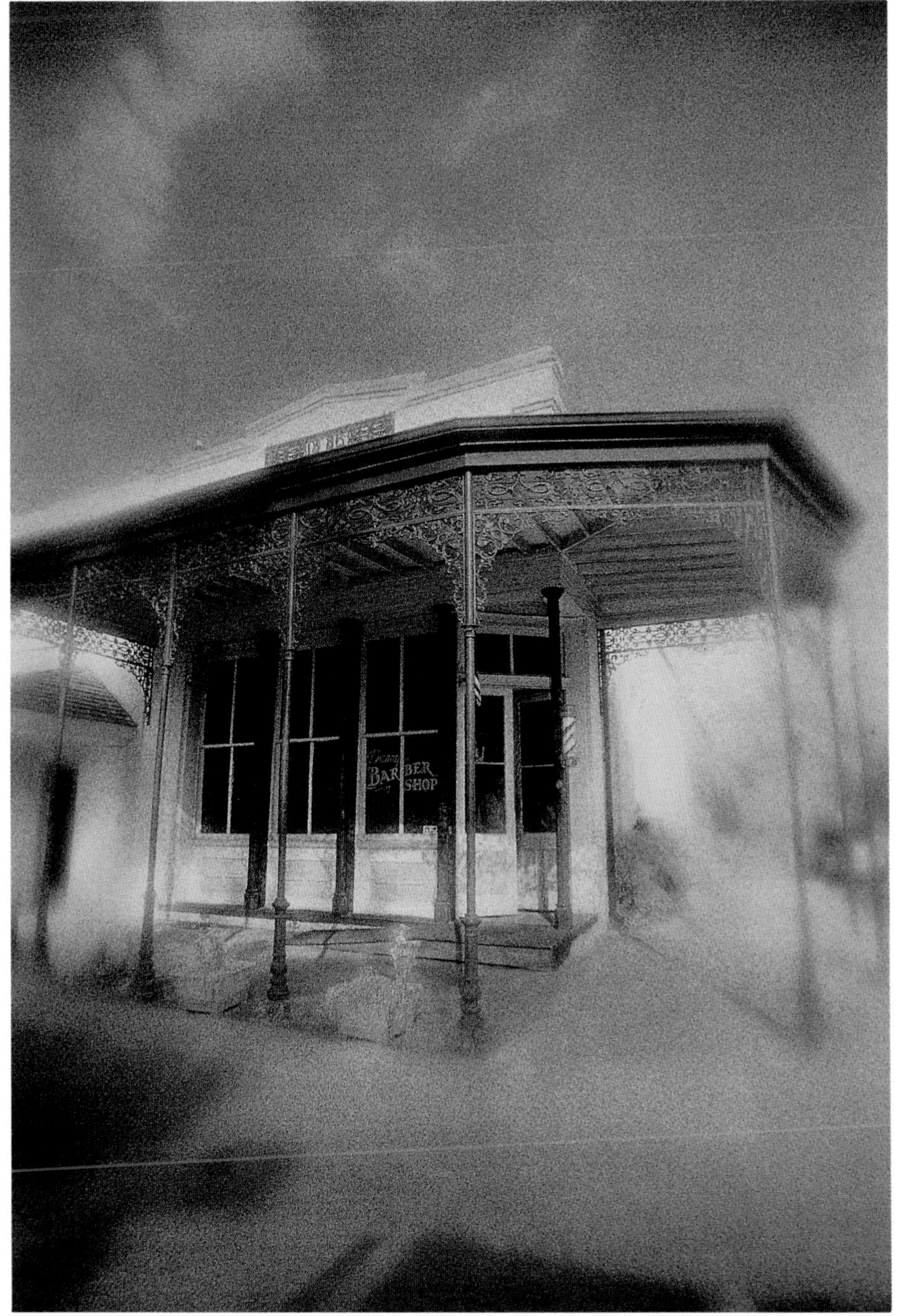
BARBER
SHOP

Only a few things were essential
at that time and place.
The way he saw it, a gun
provided wild meat, sport, a man's
security.
A cross-cut saw
provided timber for home and barn,
for chicken house, smokehouse, apple
house,
and the little two-seater the women
wanted.
So he provided and his folks
fed the chickens and fried them for
dinner,
fattened the pigs and feasted on ham,
picked apples and ate them to the core.
In and out, in and out, everything
everywhere
in and out.

They tugged at the chain,
lifted the heavy latch,
and left
the big milk can, the harness,
the checker game—with corn—
unfinished.
Outside, a scattering of autumn leaves
rustles around the iron wash pot
waiting
for spirits of the pioneers who built here,
or those who later laid up new logs,
to understand
that here once was life in
work, learning, games,
and sunlight.

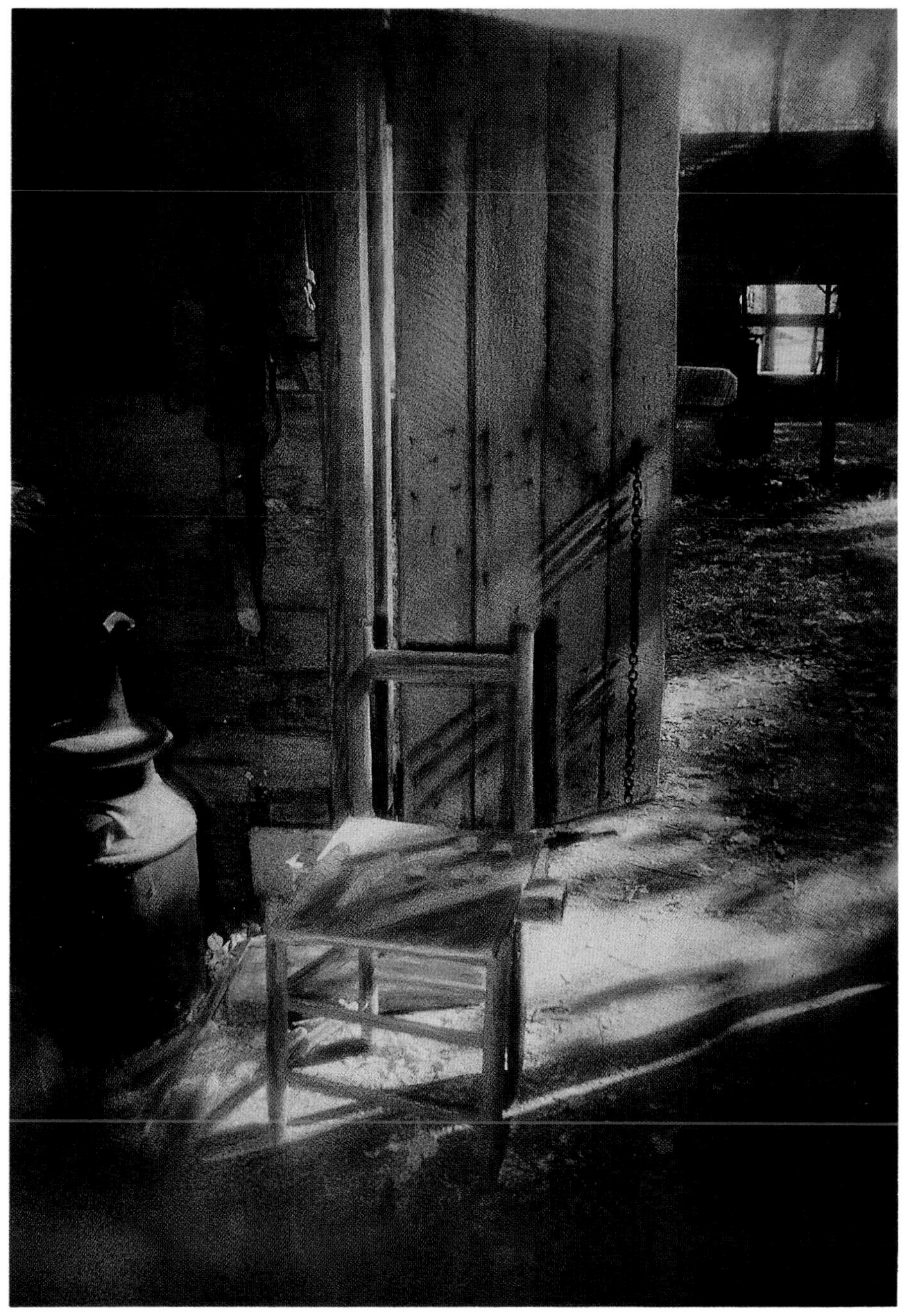

How cool it was in summer
to pass from heat and glaring sun
into its shadowy depths
and listen to the rushing stream below,
water always going somewhere else.
Under snow and rainstorm
emptied from darkening skies
these timbers held.
Shelter and safety here.

But what of that winter before the bridge
when men and women, the aged and children too,
struggled along a strange and winding trail
just here?
No shelter here for a Cherokee,
no easy way across water for a Cherokee
remembering hills and ledges, graves and rivers
of home left far behind.
And the soldiers, the guns. Everywhere.
What would home be out there
in the darkening land to the west?
Wrenched from all they knew,
cold as the chattering water,
they pressed on
like the water going somewhere else.

In those earlier days
of the place called Tennessee,
where they gathered
was not their concern,
only that they came together
in a hard time
to rediscover the faith
that brought them there,
free, oh free to worship
as they wished.
If the loft of a barn
was birthplace of a church
it reminded those who met there
that the manger of a distant
barn
sheltering quiet, patient animals,
was birthplace of The Child.

Black hands, white hands,
    separate and together,
raised a church here.

White voices, black voices,
    on alternate Sundays,
lifted hymns of praise here.

Black knees, white knees,
    bent here on different days
in prayers of thanks and suffering and
    forgiveness.

White and black, each alone,
    went home to the good earth they
    knew well.
Somewhere out there in neutral space
    did their prayers join
and rise together to the gates of heaven?

Is he here?
Was he there,
A general surprised by death?
Multiply him by five.
"It was a pleasant, hazy Indian summer day,"
the young captain wearing gray remembered,
"and so warm that I was carrying my coat on my arm."
Then the hell that was war at Franklin town erupted.
On the second day a soldier in blue
watched lines of gray sweep like a human wave
across a field where wild rabbits bounded
in a line before the army,
rabbits stopping, listening, scampering on again.
And there arose in that place coveys of quail,
thousands it seemed, rising, settling,
"Until finally they rose high in the air
and whirred off to the gray skylight of the north."

In the fields abandoned by rabbits and quail
the wounded and dead were harvested.
Floors in the McGavock house grew slippery with blood
and on the long back gallery
five generals who sat down together at breakfast that morning
lay dead together in the evening.
Multiply by hundreds those lying in the cemetery there—and elsewhere.
Is he here, a ghost?
Does he sometimes walk in hazy Indian summer's pleasant light?

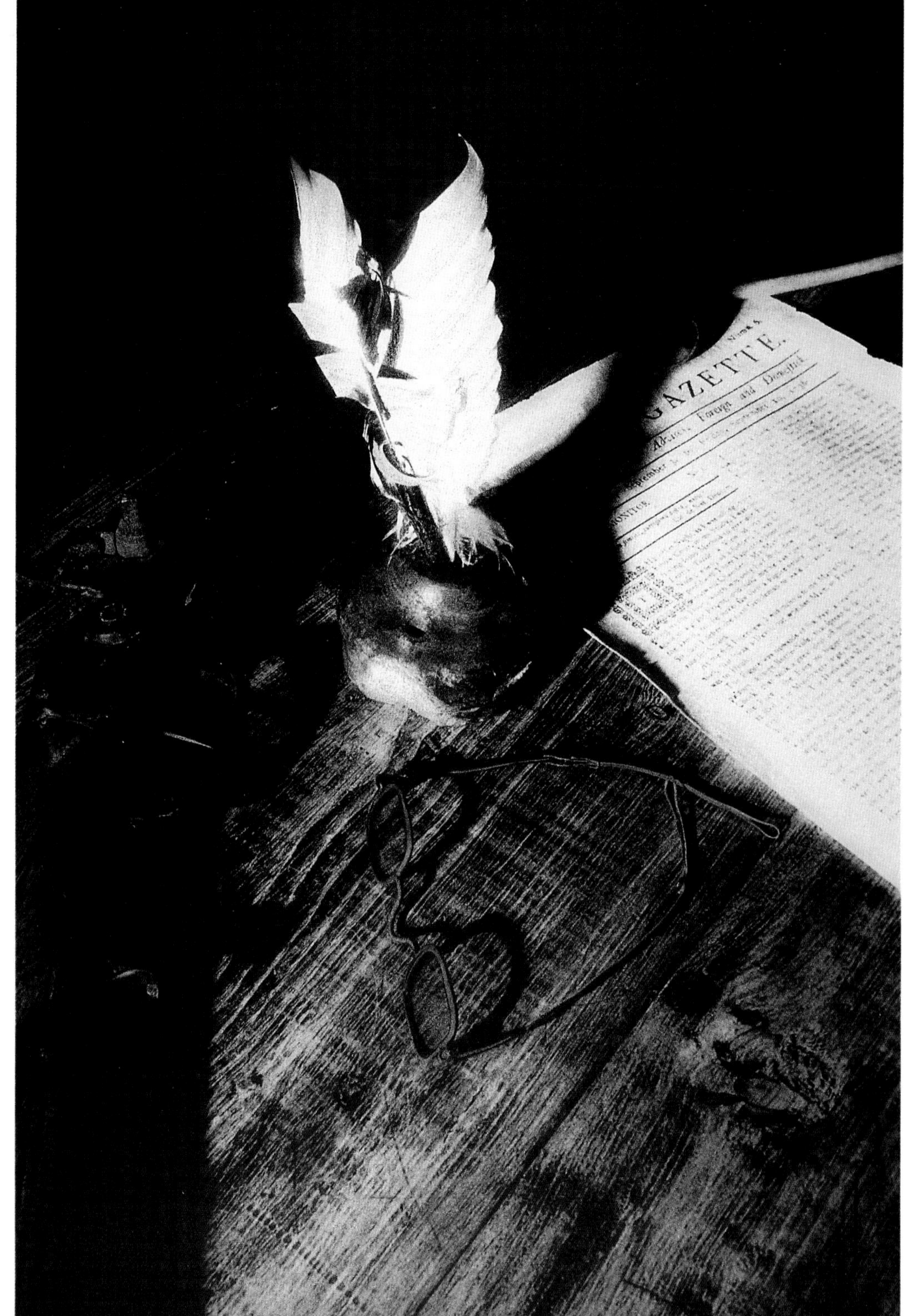

Tenasse, Tunassee, Tanasay
Explorers and soldiers fresh from Europe,
adventurers, speculators and settlers
pushing westward for new home-land,
officials assembling reports and recording deeds,
all adopted their own spelling of the flowing name given by the
Cherokees
to a river and land
they had made their own
though not by written documents of law.
Meaning of its ancient name lost to memory,
that place received new definition on
June the first, seventeen hundred and ninety-six.
Tennessee
Sixteenth of the United States of America.
And in the office of the first frame house west of the
Blue Ridge,
chiefs of Cherokee towns
and leaders from the young republic's distant capital
counseled with that governor leading a Territory
into statehood.
Glasses, *Gazette,* quill pen, quaint icons of yesterday here in
Tenasse, Tunassee, Tanasay
still speak to tomorrow
and discovery of new meanings for the name
Tennessee.

Waitin' was what they mostly did at the old gin.
Rows of wagons from first daylight to early dark
waitin' to deliver a year's cotton crop to be weighed and ginned for market.
Time for a landowner
and his sharecropper
to settle a whole year's accounts of work and debt
and what was owed each other.
The mules were good at waitin': heads bowed,
they drowsed in the heat all day as if rehearsing for a funeral.
The men traded news, familiar stories, the signs they lived by.
"Change rows while you're picking cotton, you're courting being bitten by a snake."
"Cotton falling off the wagon on the way to the gin, it's a sure sign of loss."
"Carry a baby to the field and it will grow up to be a cotton picker."
"If cotton carried to the gin isn't covered tight, a robber will steal all your money."
They grew silent, thought about that. There were several kinds of robbery.
At last, the waitin' over,
cotton weighed, worth calculated and divided,
then the tenant's debts for his share of cost of seed and fertilizer,
his family's year of wood, shelter, clothes and medicine
all deducted from his share of the cotton,
left little or no cash at all
from the year past
for the year to come.
Workin' and waitin' began all over again.
That was what they mostly did.

It was a sin,
  a mortal sin, some folks said,
to draw the bow
across the strings
and fill the air
with grief, with gladness,
whispers,
shrieks,
and laughter like sunlight coming down.
He couldn't feel the sin of it himself
but he hung his fiddle in the corner
near a fireplace
along with hot peppers on a string
and a calendar on the wall
measuring time.
But nights when the moon hung full,
or days when the air hung sweet
with clustered locust blooms and bees,
when his hands longed to clap
and his feet itched to dance,
he took the jug off the mantel
and the fiddle from the wall
and joy flowed again
as he and the fiddle
measured time.

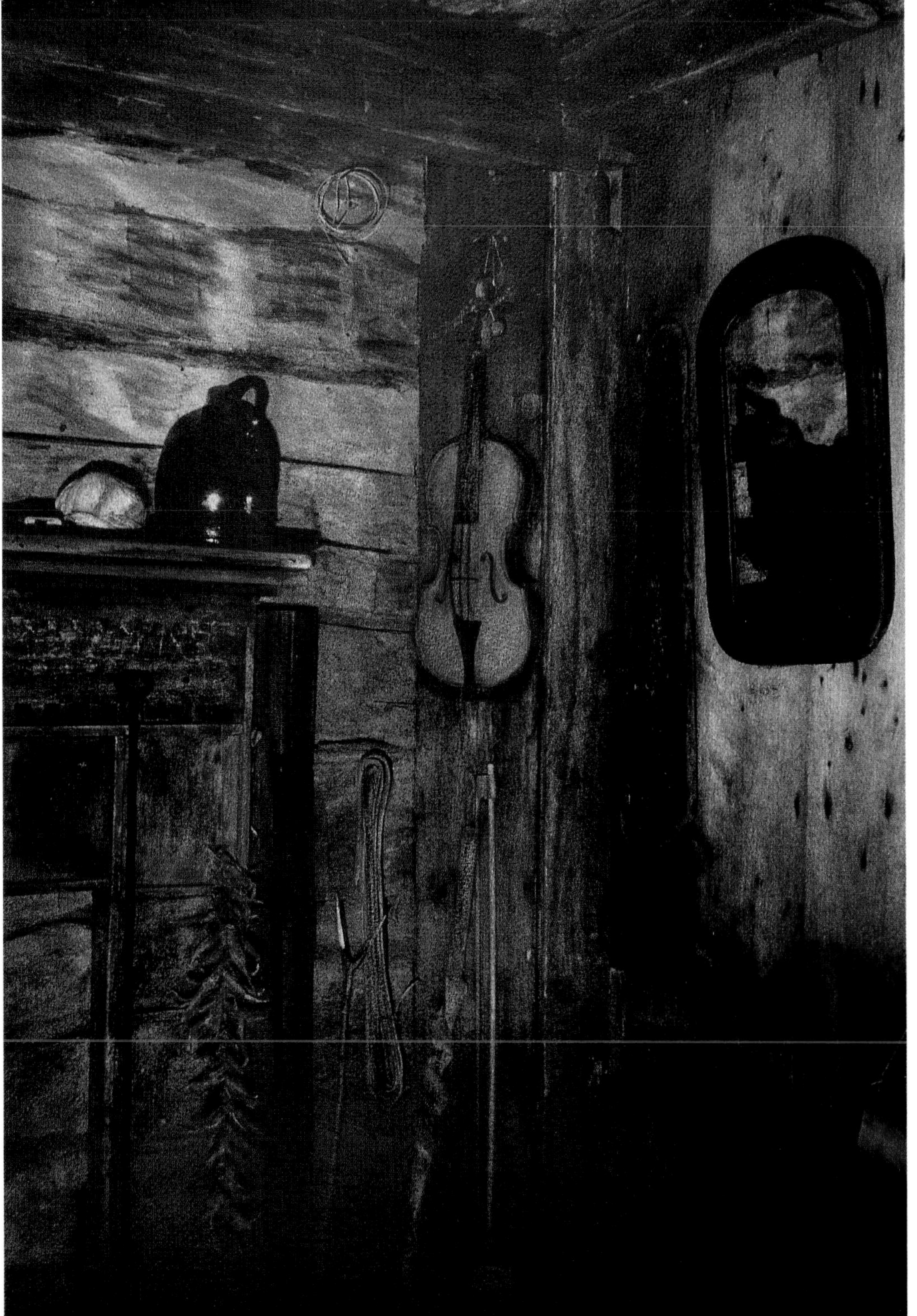

Lost in mists of time
the antique struggle, need of native
and newcomer alike
for place, for earth and woods and
waters,
struggle fierce, sad, unrelenting, costly
beyond measure.
Lost in mists of time
the names and dates of those who
huddled once
in rough-hewn cabin on this little space
terrified by tongues of fire
that leaped the fence, devoured the logs,
and finally took their brief, hopeful lives in
brutal massacre.

Now stands a later, spacious house
comfortable against the elements,
verandah and windows viewing lawn and
trees and gardens.
There are those who believe that
sometimes in the silent night
fire erupts within the dwelling.
Windows glow with ruddy flames.
If fighters of the fire arrive, their efforts
are in vain.
Strangely the flames do not consume
and it is whispered that neither fighters'
strategies nor water can contain
sparks that rise fifty feet into night skies.
When men withdraw through swinging
gate
and give a backward look—
the fire has vanished.
Thus imagination weaves mystery into
the weary pattern of our days.

Now! What manner of vehicle is this?
Its likes were never seen before
by man or beast.
What spawned it?
And why?
Some say it was constructed
to be a "prison wagon," big axles, heavy
springs,
for hauling prisoners to fields and roads
in the days of leased-out convict labor.
Some say it was a "deer wagon," took
four horses to pull it,
bringing venison back from the hunt in
days when this was wilderness.
But was it ever School Bus?
Did it truly carry young scholars
to antique classrooms
for learning rhetoric and sums and
penmanship
and Friday afternoon spelling bees?
Maybe the identity scratched there so
clearly
SCHOOL BUS
is just a memento of our folks' oldest
pastime:
playing a trick, pulling a joke
on strangers who might happen by this
shed
and wonder. Or, just maybe, was the
message
a jab in the conscience
of those in charge of the school's needs
here—even everywhere?

SCHOOL BUS

So much life in so small a space:
Loving and birthing, differing and
    dying,
Waking and sleeping,
Fetching
    wood and water,
    nature's providing.
Curing
    meat of beef and hogs
    fattened in pasture and pen,
Canning
    fruits and vegetables
    glowing like jewels in shelved jars,
Eating and drinking
    fried, boiled, baked and broiled,
    and cold milk, scalding coffee, cider,
    brandy,
Doctoring
    fevers and rashes and broken bones
    with salves and tonics from meadows
    and woods,
Sewing and mending
    clothes and quilts,
    leather of boots and shoes and
    harness,
Teaching
    the small ones by books and
    example,
Praying
    at mealtime and over the casket.
Singing and playing in summer's golden
    light.
Enduring winter's stark beauty and
    demands.
So much life in so small a space.

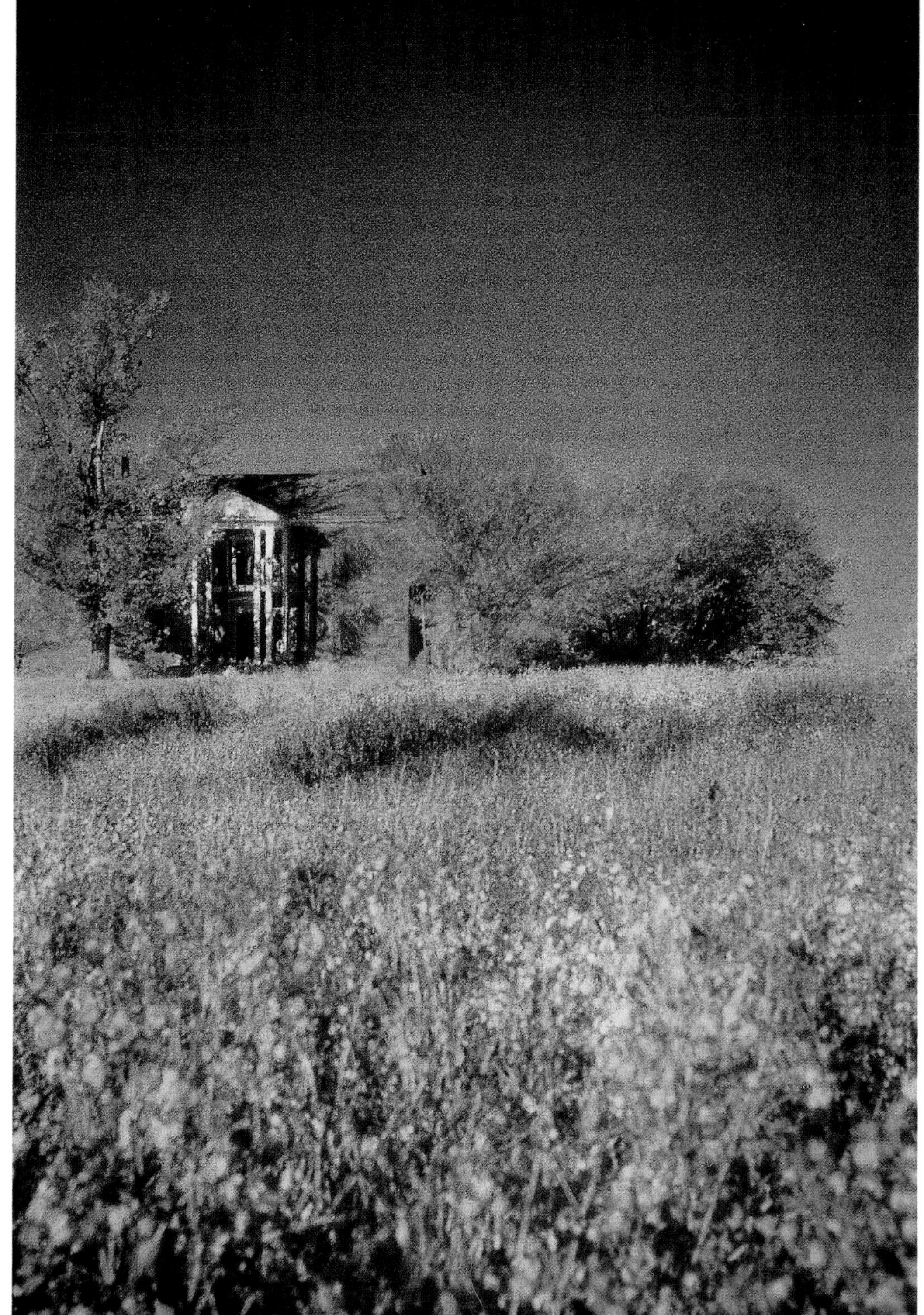

"Cotton is king," they said,
    and they were right,
those who lived in that wide half-moon
of dark, loamy earth known as the South's Black Belt.
    A king commanded servants
    and cotton had its retinue
who pushed plowshares in its fields, tended its plants, plucked
    the bolls
that yielded up their downy white treasure reluctantly.
    Through heat, drought, pestilence,
    in sweat and pain of aching backs,
cotton demanded the days and strength of their lives,
women and children no less than men in bondage to cotton.
    And here and there the fields grew
    tall houses proclaiming, "Cotton is king."

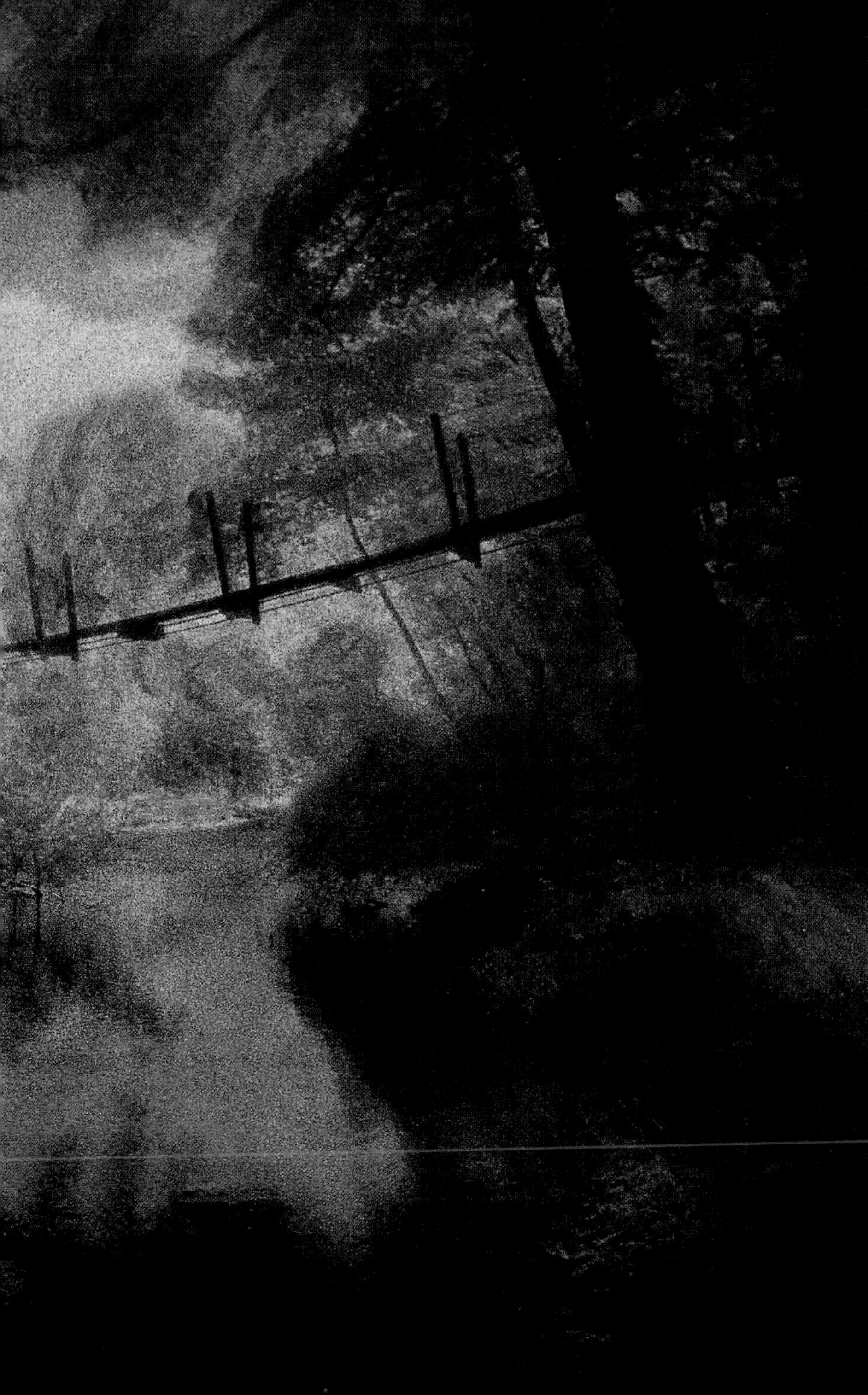

They liked the woods,
the loneliness that was not lonely
if you listened
to the voices:
wind strumming the trees,
andante, allegro, pianissimo, never the
same;
small birds busy in the thickets,
an owl mournful on a dead oak limb;
and the water
lisping gently among pebbles and grasses,
grinding stones and earth in sudden
storm,
never the same.
They liked the knowing
and the not-knowing
of all that happened
in this world they'd chosen.
And the bridge they built
was strong enough to carry them out—
if they walked just so—
and fragile enough to make a stranger
look again
at those filaments strung like a spider's
web
leading in.
The bridge served all their purposes
and they were never lonely.

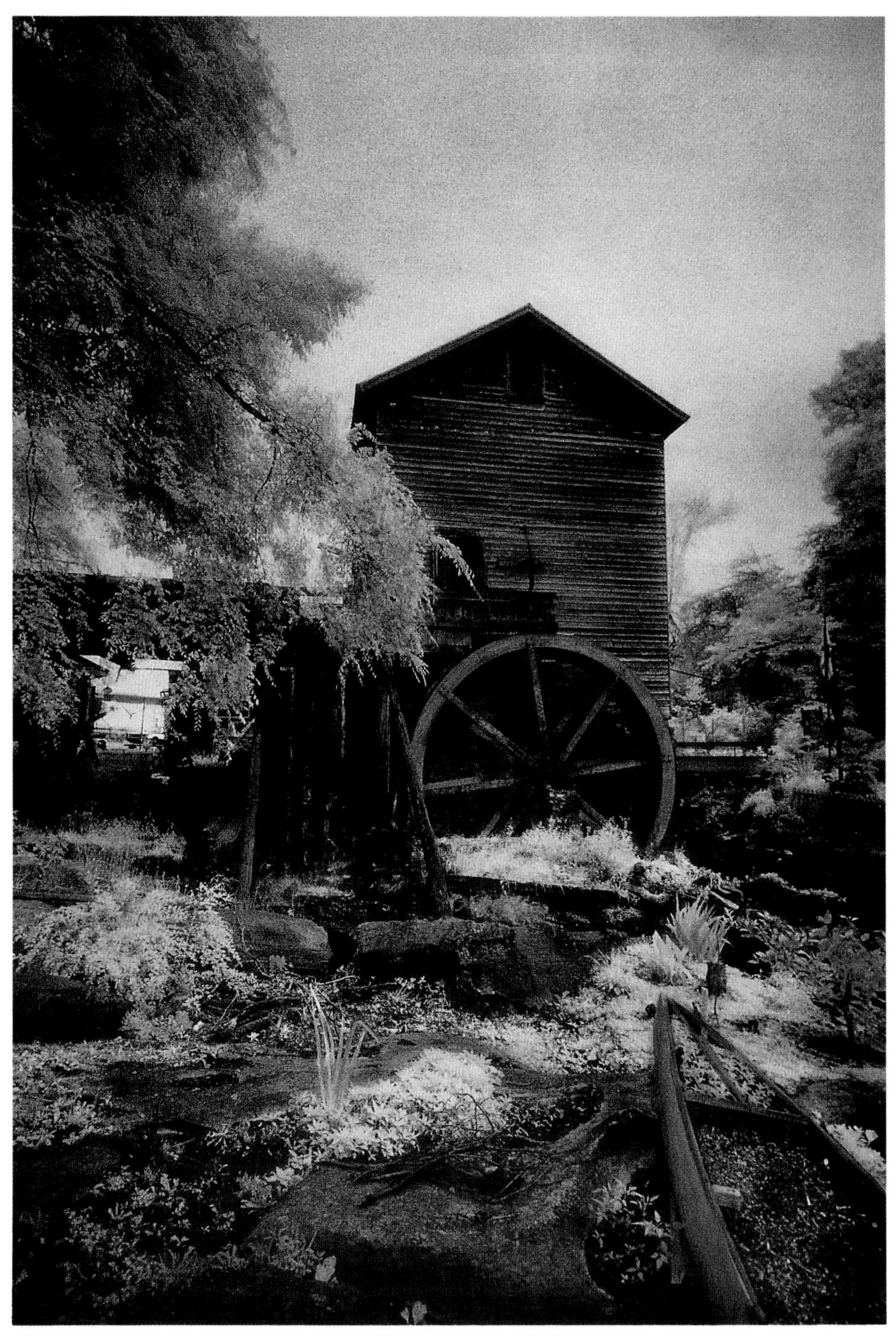

Nature determined the rhythm of life
at that place.
Stones had been a long time in the
forming,
trees had been a long time growing,
water had been a long time flowing,
before they came together
shaped into a wall, into grinding stones,
into siding and shingles and a great wheel
fed by a long, tight trough gathering the
stream's clear flow
to turn the creaking wheel outside,
and inside the heavy stone
grinding corn
into meal,
wheat
into flour.
Food.

They came with their bulging sacks from
summer's harvest
and waited their turn for the miller's
time.
Nothing could be hurried.
The water flowed,
the wheel turned,
the millstone ground, flour and meal
gathered in the bin.
Patiently the farmers' talk gathered:
neighbor's news, twice-told jokes,
political denunciations,
all grist for this welcome fellowship.
Like progress of the seasons
or procession of the constellations
life in that place turned at its own
rhythm.

The house was hers.
The barn belonged to him.
Hard-won it was, through labor of himself
and brothers, uncles, sons, neighbors.
He liked the sturdy feel of it,
the prosperous size of its top-heavy loft
protecting stalls and cribs and passageways beneath
from winter's blast,
the hot eye of summer's sun,
wind's bite and frost's sharp crunch.
Here his livestock, harness, tools and wagon,
and a random horseshoe hung above the entrance for
good luck,
were sheltered.

Where had design of such a barn been born?
Did it rise from memories that lay fallow for centuries
after moving across Russian steppes and Scandinavian forests,
German farms and settlements of the British Isles
to reach at last this Old Southwest frontier?
A strange, catch-all kind of building,
haunted by sounds of stamping hooves and bawling cows,
foraging hens and a rooster, and mice rustling
in the fragrant hay and knife-edged cornhusks in the loft
that gave its unique Tennessee shape and name to
the cantilever barn.

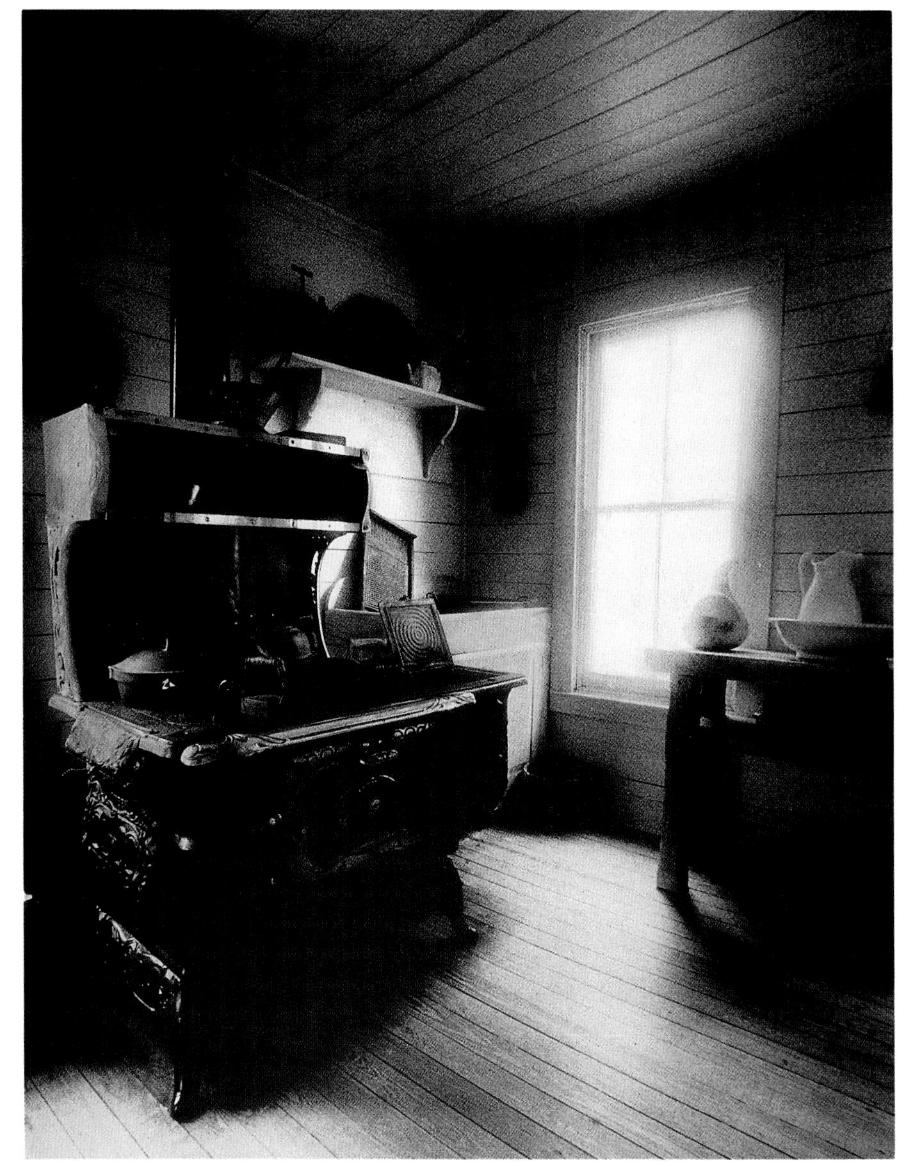

On winter mornings
smell of wood-smoke drifted
through the house
and they knew she was up and about,
feeding stove its oak and hickory sticks.
Soon the fragrance of coffee, ham and
bacon,
gold-eyed eggs straight up,
tender biscuits and juicy apples fried
would draw them down to the kitchen
where she was up and about,
feeding them.
In summer the stove yielded rich aromas:
wild berries she had picked
becoming juicy cobblers,
tomatoes she had gathered
becoming spicy ketchup.
Thanksgiving and Christmas the stove
steamed and baked and boiled and
simmered
the bounty she offered family and friend
and stranger alike.
When she died
no one seemed to know the magic
of drafts and vents and the lidded
warmer and temperamental oven.
Stove sat there,
cold.

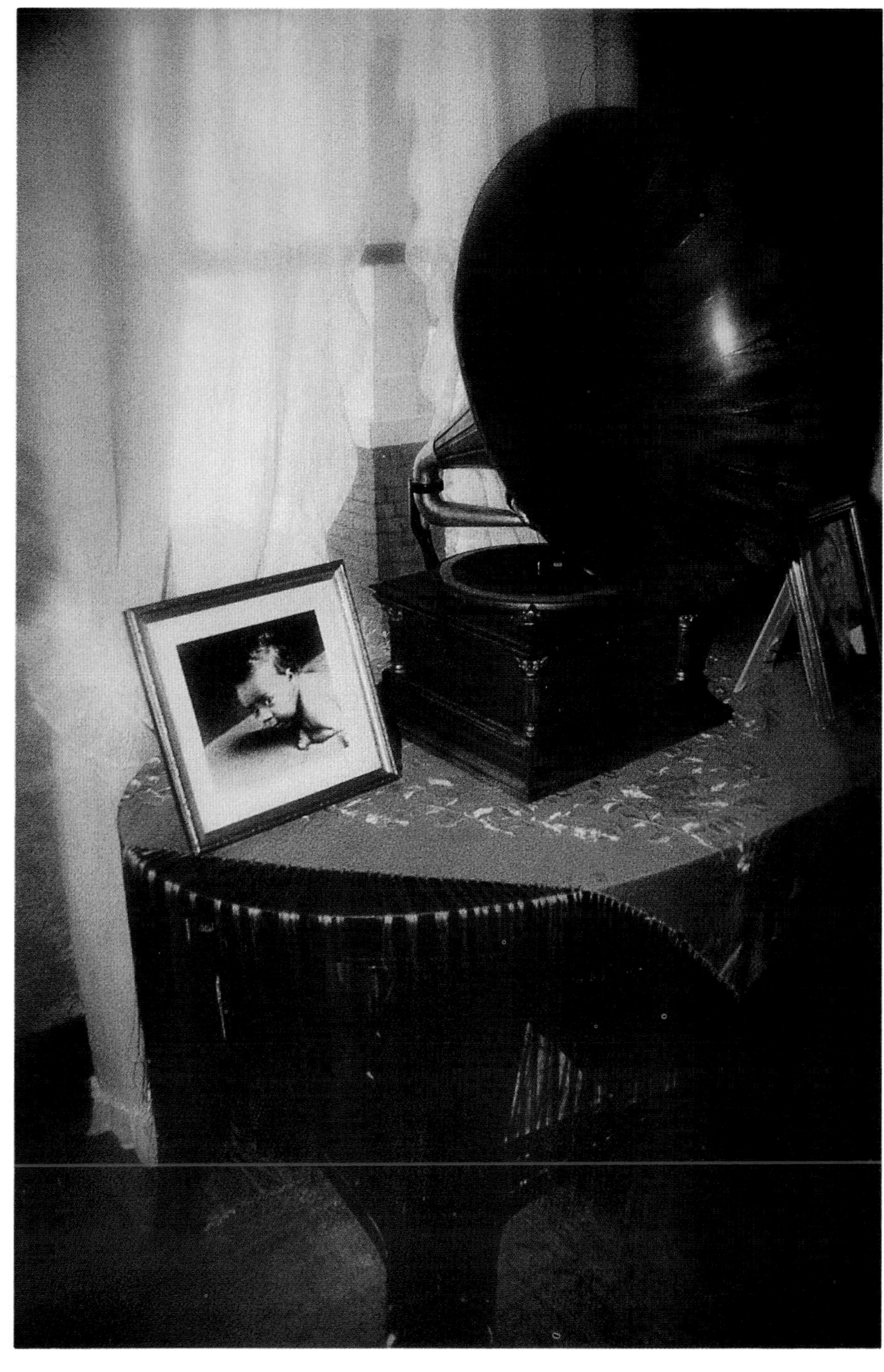

His bright eyes
    Looked—and watched.
  His young ears
Listened—and heard.
  The old ones spoke
Memories.
  The young ones shared
Dreams.
  From deep Roots
the story of a people blossomed
and reached around the world.

The earth trembled.
Hillsides tumbled,
swallowed in a great depression.
December sixteenth, 1811.
Roosters crowed at midnight.
Streams changed course.
People thought of Pentecost
and prayed.
The earth shook—
did not settle for three long months.
People packed their household goods
on wagons and carriages
and set out for Someplace Else.
The mammoth Mississippi reversed itself,
surged into the wide emptiness of land
and from the earthquake's crater made a lake.
When all the shocks had settled,
folks moved back,
named the quiet lake Reelfoot
after a crippled chief of Creeks or Cherokees
who once walked this land.
When the earth trembles
it's wise to remember all the spirits
that may dwell there.

Sometimes folks hurried
across the nearby field.
Mostly they ambled
along the well-worn road
that was more like a path
leading to the store
that carried a few of everything
anybody might need
to see them through the day.
And there was a porch for shade
to sit and whittle or drink a coke and talk.
After a while the county paved the road
and things moved faster, taking some folks into town.
He had to publish his name.
Then the government laid down an Interstate
long and smooth as a snake uncoiling across the
countryside,
nowhere near his store.
He knew about Progress though:
set out his antique scales and knick-knacks for y'all
and became a Museum.
He hated to put bars over the windows.
But he guessed progress had its price.
Strangers everywhere.

WELCOME
Y'ALL
PLUMMERS GRO
Coca-Cola

It was a long strange way
from that hill called Kings Mountain on
the border between two Carolinas
to the Upper Cumberland River country
in the land of the Western Waters.
Tilman Dixon was there that October
day
Seventeen-hundred-and-eighty, A.D.
when the Over-Mountain men
broke one wing of confident Cornwallis's
army,
shattered British dreams of holding their
rebellious colonies.
Land was his reward,
good land near the Indian boundaries.

That ancient tool, the broad-axe, once an
iron-age weapon,
smoothed and smoothed and smoothed
the great rough logs
and an eight-room house and barns and
smaller dependencies arose.
Pack-horses carried feather-beds and
laces into the wilderness,
brought hats and shoes and niceties
and a future King of France to visit
the tavern-keeper, merchant, postmaster,
magistrate,
Builder of school, keeper of court (good
whiskey and brandy 2 1/2 cents the
half-pint).

And on the hempen rope laced across
the bottom of the sturdy bed
did he awaken sometimes in the downy
comfort of feather-bed and pillows
and think he smelled wet leaves,
gunpowder and fresh blood
in the October woods?
What had taken him there? What
brought him here?
How long ago it was—and strange.

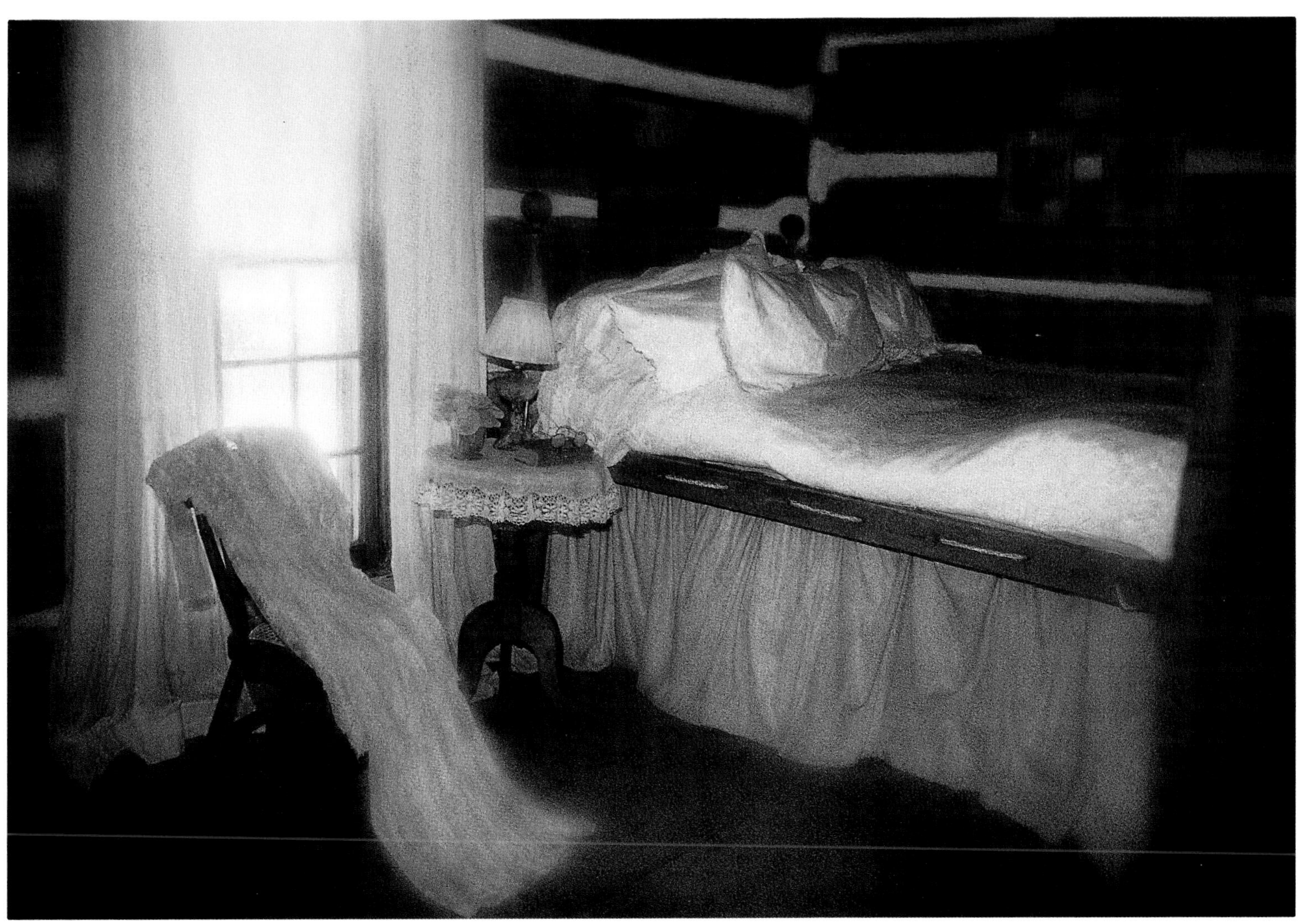

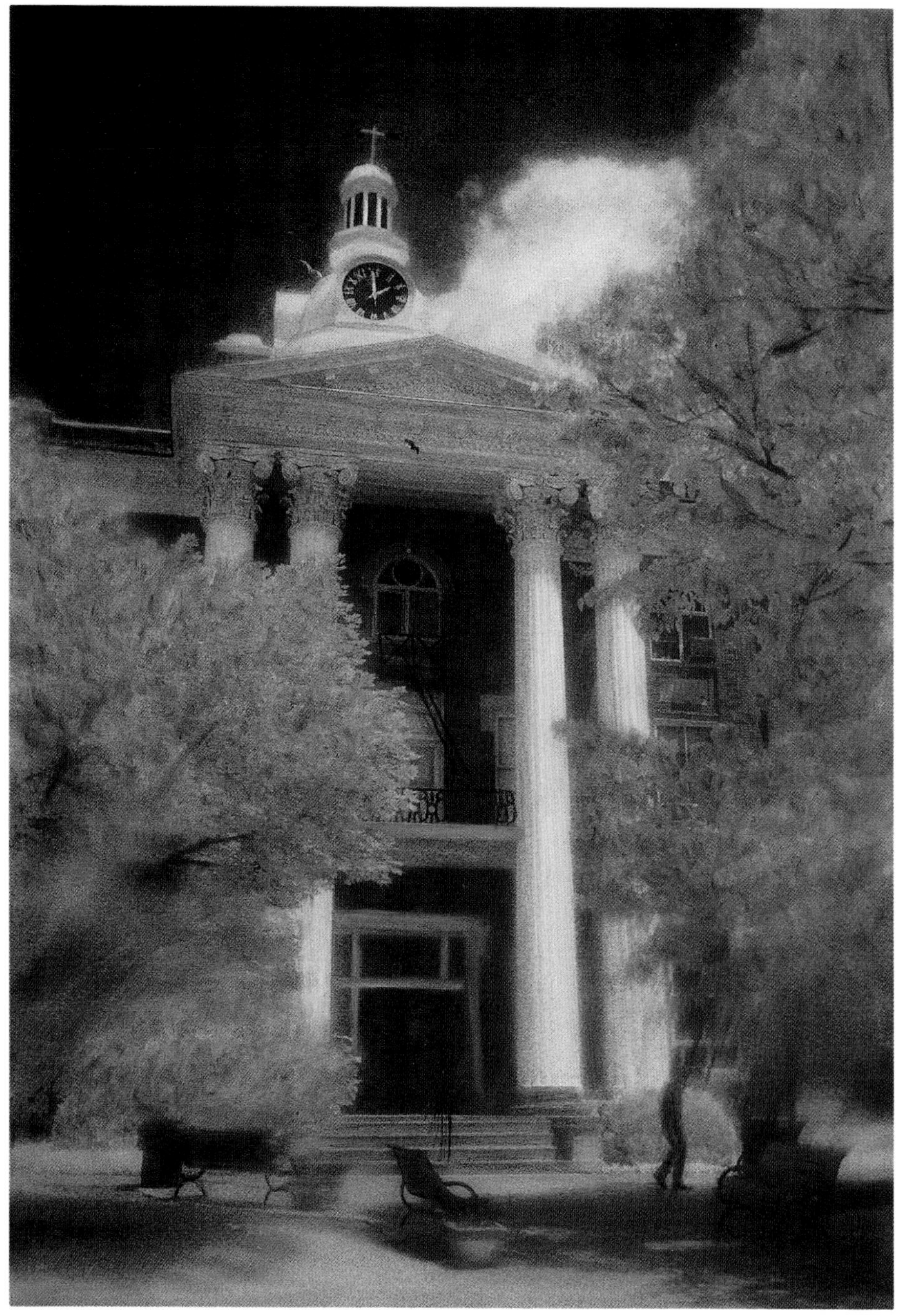

Births—
 and deaths
Marriages—
 and deeds
Taxes—
 and licenses
  to floorboard a Chevy down the Interstate,
  run a business (into the ground, an uncle warned)
  send Old Blue baying after the fox under a hunter's
 moon.
Life logged here.

Theft—and
 weeping for someone's bicycle; a family inheritance;
 mementos.
Lies—
 casting nets of deceit beyond recall.
Murder—and
 pain deeper than any wound of knife or bullet.
Evil weighed and debated here.

A country's weakness or nobility
 right here.
Justice in this place.

He knew this job carried a lot of
responsibility.
He took it seriously,
kept the planks in floor and table
scrubbed,
made sure there was oil in lamp inside,
lantern outside,
had titles on the door
printed in that fancy English script.
Much as he liked the excitement and the
power,
being where things happened,
he resented it when there was mud and
vomit
and blood.

But sometimes when there was no one
else around
and the street outside lay quiet as dust
and even the jar-flies were too lazy to
raise a noise,
he'd talk to the man in the cage
(he didn't hold with jailing women).
After all, the prisoner was still a man
and if truth was known
probably no meaner than many a one
walking free outside.
Sometimes they told him stories he'd
never heard before.
Even a sheriff
needed companionship.

How promising was that spring
  in the fields and camps of Tennessee,
and nowhere lovelier
than at the pond
where water reflected sky and clouds,
and in the rows of orchard
where a burst of pink bloom foretold
heavy harvest of succulent peaches.
How promising was that spring
when they gathered
from farms and villages and cities,
faces shining with youth and belief
before the thud of cannon fire
broke a Sunday morning calm
and they marched out arranged
in rows as neat as peach trees,
an orchard of men who fell,
turned cool water into a Bloody Pond,
transformed the Peach Orchard into a
  shroud
of trampled petals, slain trees and soldiers
  side by side.
Peaches taken in their season of blossoms
before summer's ripening,
young men harvested in their springtime—
at Shiloh.

Suppose a building is
architecturally a "woods colt"
of uncertain parentage,
a strange, arresting building.
Suppose it passes early years
in postal service for the U.S.A.
and its reincarnation comes
as office of an electric company
and finally there are empty years of
waiting
until its purpose is discovered:
to serve as haven for the past,
home to history's story.
History as varied and inviting,
as hidden and mysterious,
as dark and bright,
as frightening and bountiful
and yet to be explored
as the strange, woods-colt building it
inhabits.

Tracks, they were called:
iron rails laid along the valleys,
through mountains, beside the rivers.
Nothing like it here before.
They were not tracks
left by those
who first stamped trails through wilderness,
paws and hooves and claws
beating back and forth
seeking water, food and shelter,
engineering paths the rails would follow.
And the men who laid that iron
carried memories in blood and bone
of Africa's suns, Ireland's peat-bogs,
and hunger for land, adventure, hope
that sent the trains thundering from sea to sea.

The engines bellowed, whistled long, loud wails,
and billowed clouds of steam
as the wheels screeched to a halt
at stations perched beside the track.
Horses reared and snorted and tried to run,
old folks shook their heads, called them "the cars"
and marveled at the destinations of this magic carpet
carrying strangers in.
After awhile strangers became natives who
rode the train out, sometimes
seeking the way to ancient lands
of those who laid the tracks here.

COWAN

Moving on.
They worked tar into the heavy,
creaking wheels,
stretched a cover over the wagon's
naked ribs
and rolled westward.
Always west.
Moving on.
It was what they did
when fire devoured or flood assaulted
or fever carried away
all they had called home
for a little space of time.
He did a lot of moving on—
Greene County to Jefferson when he
was seven or eight,
hired out at twelve on a cattle-drive to
Virginia,
more youthful rambling until marriage
and a family tied him to one place.
(The cabin was less permanent than the
wagon—out there waiting.)
High rent and restlessness
untied that knot.
The wagon rolled on to Lincoln County,
to Franklin County,
to Lawrence County at the head of Shoal
Creek.
160 acres of land, neat cabin, grist mill,
powder mill, distillery.
Public office: justice of the peace, colonel
of militia, state legislator.
Roots.
"Swept away all to smash" by a summer
freshet that left only debts
and a wife who said, "Just pay up and we
will scuffle for more."
The wagon rolled again
moving on to Obion in the Jackson
purchase
and at last to the Alamo.
The cabin and the wagon equal partners
in history.

Follow the slow way home
and hear the voices:
wind strums through limbs of deep-
rooted trees,
cocky rooster proclaims his flock's
foraging,
cool water splashes in trough and tub
to quench perpetual thirst of plants and
creatures.
Cross beyond the railroad's intrusion
and enter a place where people live
close upon the nurtured earth
that feeds them,
with calm animals
that serve them,
in tidy buildings
that shelter them,
where people hang Monday's wash
to dry in fresh sweet air
beneath trees and sky,
making home
one wide embrace of all creation that is
this place.

List of Illustrations